THE TRAVELLERS

A PLAY IN THREE ACTS

Rajeshwar Prasad

TSL Drama

THE TRAVELLERS

A Play In Three Acts

A railway platform in cold December 2017. CECIL and BLAIR are sitting on a concrete bench waiting for a train. Behind them is a signboard "Welcome to MISSLAND – the town where nothing is as it seems".

Their train is delayed because of a sudden unexpected incident which has damaged the tracks.

While BLAIR goes to the pharmacy, ALVIN arrives and begins talking to CECIL.

It's a busy station with some passengers roaming, some sitting at coffee shops, some talking, some watching the television screens. Vendors, customers, stalls including a flower seller.

An announcement is heard. *"Passengers, attention please! The Superfast Express . . . is running late by about an hour because of damage to the tracks. The inconvenience caused is deeply regretted."*

Running Time

50 minutes

Characters

Cecil	*50 year old, Managing Director in a diamond factory*
Blair	*50 year old, traveller with Cecil*
Alvin	*30 year old, permanent transient*
Newsreader	*pre-recorded news bulletin*

Setting

A busy mainline train platform
in December 2017

Act 1

Lights up.

CECIL and BLAIR are sitting on a bench on the railway platform.

An announcement is heard: "Passengers, attention please! The Superfast Express . . . is running late by about an hour because of damage to the tracks. The inconvenience caused is deeply regretted."

CECIL: The train is late by about an hour today . . . absolutely unexpected. We will reach our destination very late.

BLAIR: Of course! Due to damage to the tracks, completely unexpected, most trains are running late.

CECIL: It is too cold today. We are shivering. [*Shivers*]

BLAIR: Every year we have to face the same situation in December and January.

CECIL: The end of the year means suffering – similar to the end of life.

BLAIR: And old age is of the same vein. January is the beginning of the year, but it is cold like December. Its coldness is tolerable because we live in expectation that after January cold will decrease. But it continues to come and go each year. Finally, December comes. The end of the year is like the end of life – the beginning of the year and the end of the year – the beginning of life and the end of life.

CECIL:	It is a record cold day this year.
BLAIR:	Each year we say the same. Time passes and the summer arrives. Youth departs, and old age beckons.
CECIL:	I am not feeling it is fine weather today.
BLAIR:	Either one likes or dislikes, it'll go on. Life is the name of this and that.
CECIL:	In this way, time passes away. We fail to follow.
BLAIR:	All is right.
	[*Long pause*]
CECIL:	Really, untouchables are filthy. They are unlike men. Animals are better than them. There is no meaning to their life.
BLAIR:	They are men like us. But they are different in colour and race. Their culture is different.
CECIL:	I understand all this.
BLAIR:	All of us are separated by colour, caste, religion, sect, race, sex, nationality, but we are the same.
CECIL:	The world is really wonderful. Men are different, but their blood is the same. The colour of blood does not differ.
BLAIR:	God has made the world. How wonderful!
CECIL:	Really!
BLAIR:	God is just. God is almighty, the One who gives us everything.
CECIL:	He also gives and takes – sends and calls.
BLAIR:	Everything given by God is snatched once.
CECIL:	This is a part of the mysterious working of God.
BLAIR:	God gives – God snatches. We continue to see.
CECIL:	God gives and takes more or less to everyone.
BLAIR:	God has given us everything. We're at the same level. Our income is also near about.

CECIL:	We are really fortunate.
BLAIR:	Right!
CECIL:	There is a man in my neighbourhood who pines even for food. He tried hard to earn and live like me, but lost everything through business. He was once a manager in a five star hotel.
BLAIR:	It is written in his fate. Let him pine. We are fortunate.
CECIL:	Yes! Misfortunes have embraced him.
BLAIR:	Misfortunes never come alone.
CECIL:	Right you are.
	[*Long pause*]
BLAIR:	Today, I got up early because I had to get the train with you. All in vain. The train is late.
CECIL:	I am feeling uneasy because of the delay of the train.
BLAIR:	All around! Man has the same condition.
CECIL:	Sometimes, trains are late – sometimes tracks are broken – sometimes engines fail – sometimes roads are jammed – the chains of uneasiness – problems all around us.
BLAIR:	We witness winter after the rainy season – spring after winter, and summer after spring.
CECIL:	We witness different phases and stages of time and things.
BLAIR:	Really.
CECIL:	Wonders and wonders!
BLAIR:	Everywhere!
CECIL:	Wonders, but life continues to go on.
BLAIR:	I am tired because I went to sleep late and got up early.

CECIL :	Now you can sleep on this bench for some time or till the train comes.
BLAIR:	My digestion is also not good today.
CECIL:	Perhaps you have had too much oily and spicy food.
BLAIR:	No.
CECIL:	I guess.
BLAIR:	No! Lack of proper rest at night.
CECIL:	Yes! Yes! Rest is very necessary in life.
BLAIR:	No rest, no life.
CECIL:	You should take something for it.
BLAIR:	I think there are some antacid tablets in your bags.
CECIL:	Yes! They are in a packet in my bag.
BLAIR:	In which packet?
CECIL:	In the red bag.
	[*BLAIR unchains the bag and takes out the packet. They take out a bottle*]
BLAIR:	It's expired.
CECIL:	[*Surprised*] Expired?
BLAIR:	Yes.
CECIL:	Throw it.
	[*BLAIR throws it in the nearby dustbin*]
BLAIR:	I have a dilemma: what to do and what not to do.
CECIL:	You should get something from the pharmacy.
BLAIR:	Okay. I'll go.
CECIL:	Okay.
	BLAIR leaves.
	Lights down.

Act 2

Lights up.

CECIL is alone on the platform.

A man in old garments and with a pale face approaches.

He stands opposite CECIL.

ALVIN: I have to travel by the train which is to arrive on this platform.

CECIL: You are talking about which train? I have to travel by the Superfast. Do you?

ALVIN: I forget the destination. But I know all travel by the same train. All have come from the same place. All go to the same place.

CECIL: A wonder! You forget even the place to which you have to travel, and you are unnecessarily talking.

ALVIN: I frequently forget but I try to remember.

CECIL: But I never forget. I save it in mind. My mind is a super computer.

ALVIN: It may be, but I don't believe.

CECIL: Either you believe or not, but I never forget.

ALVIN: Tell me about the train.

CECIL: No train has departed under an hour.

ALVIN: No train? [*Laughingly*] At each moment trains come and carry travellers to their destination.

CECIL: O great fool! You're laughing without any reason. I've been waiting for a train for an hour. But all trains are running late which is frequently announced by the announcer. You can also listen to it. Wait for some time.

[*Off stage. "Passengers, attention please! The Superfast Express . . . is running late by about an hour. The inconvenience caused is deeply regretted."*]

ALVIN: Trains may run late but man runs on time, which is unknown by anyone in this world.

CECIL: I don't understand. What do you mean to say?

ALVIN: Obviously, no one understands.

CECIL: I am not like others. I am a post-graduate in science. I can solve any mathematical question posed for me. Test me. Ask any question from anywhere and from any science field. I am one of the best from the *University of Wonderland*. I got several awards. I have medals are in my bag which you can see, if you wish.

ALVIN: I have seen many medals in my life though I have won nothing, nor have I any interest to win because I know the best medal for life is death which is definitely won once, but unknown by the winners.

CECIL: I do not understand all this. I am satisfied with . . . what I have got. I have gained all this because of my hard labour.

ALVIN: All is meaningless.

CECIL: Views differ. Ideas differ. Man to man. Man and himself. This is not a matter of debate.

[*Keeping his hands on his shoulders, in friendly fashion, ALVIN addresses CECIL*]

ALVIN   I think you have to go to Willshire.

CECIL   No. I've to go to Pityland.

ALVIN: Where?

CECIL: Pityland. And you?

ALVIN: I've to go, [*Sadly*] but I forget the name of the place.

CECIL: [*Surprised*] It is a wonder that a man forgets the name of the place where he has to go. If he forgets his place, how will he reach his destination?

ALVIN: All of us forget our place.

CECIL: And to which place do you belong?

ALVIN: I forget my homeland too.

CECIL: [*Surprised*] You forget your homeland too?!

ALVIN: [*Slowly and sadly*] Yes.

CECIL: [*Surprised*] How's that so you forget?!

ALVIN: This is a common thing. You also forget. All forget.

CECIL: Never! My memory is stable. I return even after a long time from anywhere. I can move round the world alone without any confusion.

ALVIN: I don't believe.

CECIL: But I see and experience.

ALVIN: This is fact. We have loss of memory. We always lose, never gain.

CECIL: But I know.

ALVIN: You know nothing.

CECIL: I know you. Be seated here.

            [*CECIL moves his luggage for ALVIN to sit*]

ALVIN: Thanks. [*Sits beside CECIL*]

CECIL: What is your profession? It seems that you are a loiterer.

ALVIN: We all are permanent loiterers.

CECIL: No!

ALVIN: This is only fact.

CECIL: You are a child.

ALVIN:	I am not a child.
CECIL:	You're a child, but not in age, rather in knowledge.
ALVIN:	All are ignorant – all are naturally childish in knowledge.
CECIL:	All are different.
ALVIN:	You do not understand.
CECIL:	All do according to their intellectual and physical condition – they gain – they lose.
ALVIN:	All is right. But its final run ends with death. In this way, all become equal. There is neither difference nor reservation – neither priority nor security.
CECIL:	It seems . . . that you are . . .
ALVIN:	What?
CECIL:	You have not attended any school, so you have no knowledge.
ALVIN:	No! I have attended.
CECIL:	Where?
ALVIN:	I attended my village school.
CECIL:	But you have learnt nothing.
ALVIN:	I tried hard, but . . .
CECIL:	You have not worked hard to know and learn.
ALVIN:	I tried ever so hard, but failed everywhere. [Sadly] So, now I am a lone loiterer.
CECIL:	I can know anyone without asking questions. I knew you were a loiterer. I want to let you know. "Failed" means "you failed at school".
ALVIN:	[Sadly] Everywhere, not only at school.
CECIL:	[Surprisingly] Everywhere?!
ALVIN:	[Sadly] Yes, everywhere!
CECIL:	Really, a unique creature you are. You are a wonderful being!

ALVIN: I can't understand any matter of any teachers – what did he say? They said, "Life . . . love . . . hate . . . mercy . . . compassion . . . plus . . . minus . . . God . . . Nature . . . "

CECIL: But, of course! I have enough experience of all this. I have ever topped – first class first. Teachers loved me and blessed me heartily. I was one of the favourite ones. I am of and by their blessings. I thought enough. They were happy with me.

ALVIN: There is no meaning in their blessings. They have blessed you, but who had blessed them? Had they been blessed by anyone? And the blessing persons had been blessed by whom?

CECIL: They had been blessed, and they had blessed, and blessed and blessed – they are blessing.

ALVIN: They will not continue to bless forever.

CECIL: But they will till the end of their life.

ALVIN: And after the end of their life?

CECIL: Naturally . . . !

ALVIN: They are not alive, whoever had blessed them. What has been left by them? What happened to blessing ones . . . blessed ones . . . what will happen further?

CECIL: [*Very slowly and sadly*] But . . . we . . . all . . . live in the same way . . .

ALVIN: The fact is that you are not satisfied with whatever you have.

CECIL: I am satisfied.

ALVIN: Now you may think the meaning of blessings is meaningless. You have nothing.

CECIL: [*Happily*] I have many things! I have a villa in Gold Colony and around it crossroads. The neighbourhood has all the facilities of the age – a school, a college, a university, a telephone exchange, a post office, a hi-fi hospital and all others in my neighbourhood – A to Z before my house which I use and enjoy. We live happily. It seems that it is heaven on earth. Amid all this, there is my shining and sparkling villa which is gold-coated. Everything is there.

[*Pause*]

ALVIN: Your pose shows you are married.

CECIL: Yes! I'm a married man.

ALVIN: I think you have proved your manliness.

CECIL: [*Angrily*] I am not impotent like you.

ALVIN: No. I'm sorry. I am not an impotent man.

CECIL: Yes! I've proved.

ALVIN: And how many child . . . ren . . . ?

CECIL: Average good in number.

ALVIN: Four . . . five . . . six . . . ?

CECIL: The proper number of the age and phase.

ALVIN: Now you don't like to increase?

CECIL: No.

ALVIN: Your wife also doesn't like to have . . .

CECIL: Don't cross the limit. That is entirely not your matter.

ALVIN: [*Begs pardon*] Have your parents died?

CECIL: Yes, they have passed away.

ALVIN: You will follow your parents' departure.

CECIL: [*Very sadly*] Let the time come.

ALVIN: You must think about the time when death comes.

CECIL: [*Becomes sad*] Oh . . . Time knows.

ALVIN: It means, you decline the eternal fact.

CECIL: [*Very sadly*] Let the time come.

ALVIN:	Time does not wait for anything or anyone in any way.
CECIL:	[*Sadly*] That is for all, not only for me.
ALVIN:	One has to adopt the same path as has been adopted by one's forefathers. We have . . .
CECIL:	[*Keeping both hands on his head*] You are an escapist. It seems.
ALVIN:	No!
CECIL:	But it seems.
ALVIN:	I am not an escapist.
	[*Pause*]
	But I feel I am a permanent transient. My father married thrice and issued seven children. But he lives with no one. He lives alone in a government camp for the poor. My mother divorced my father and married another, a young and handsome man who satisfies her lust enough. I meet her who loves me enough, but for the time being. After some time, she says to me to earn to live – to work hard for my survival – to marry a woman but not to live with her. Her love for me is for only sometime. Finally, she says to go work and settle my own family and business.
CECIL:	If your mother doesn't love you, your father will definitely love.
ALVIN:	No! My father also does not allow me to live with him. When I meet him, he blesses saying "live long" – showing his love for me, and then he says to return to settle anywhere – wherever I find suitable.
CECIL:	But my parents said not to leave them, and whenever I went anywhere even for a day, they began to search for me. For my security.
ALVIN:	Oh! For security? It means you were not secured.

CECIL:	This was his duty because he had more experiences of life than me.
ALVIN:	Whatsoever? But not my father or mother.
CECIL:	I feel he is an illiterate.
ALVIN:	Yes!
CECIL:	It seems your mother is also illiterate.
ALVIN:	You are right. She is also an illiterate. But they have deep knowledge of the world and Nature. They are absolutely Nature-lettered.
CECIL:	But they do not know society.
ALVIN:	They also know society. But they did so and so, and say that they are right and doing everything naturally.
CECIL:	You should live with your wife.
ALVIN:	I am a man without wife.
CECIL:	Aha you are an unmarried lad!
ALVIN:	Yes.
CECIL:	So, you have no sexual relations with any woman at all.
ALVIN:	No. It was in the past.
CECIL:	Aha! You have undertaken sex acts with a woman?
ALVIN:	Yes.
CECIL:	You have done, so you have enjoyed enough.
ALVIN:	No, only two or three times.
CECIL:	With whom?
ALVIN:	With a woman at the beggars' park.
CECIL:	You should marry her and continue.
ALVIN:	Now she lives away from me.
CECIL:	She is not licking your sex organ. Tell her to lick.
ALVIN:	She left me because I could not satisfy her.

CECIL: If you are impotent, no woman will allow you to have sex acts. You must know all this.

ALVIN: No, I am not impotent, rather she was an elephant – above sixty in age and above a hundred in weight – too lustful in craze.

CECIL: You are hiding from reality. I understand all this. Please share your experiences if you have done so.

ALVIN: She used to sleep in the same shed made for beggars, in which I used to sleep. One night when the light was switched off due to some technical fault, she came under my quilt. She began to rub her breast to my cheeks. Then she forwarded her hands to my sex organ. So it was excited. Later, she took me upon her placing my sex organ at her sex organ, and I did as I could. After some moments she came upon me and took me under her thighs and began to press as much as I was to be crushed and ground by her thighs and a strong body, though she was over sixty. It seemed I was fully within her. My sex organ began to ache. The next day, she repeated the same act. I was really happy that at least I had one with whom I can share my findings. The third day, she began to do the same but I failed to satisfy her. So, she abused me saying "brother-in-law . . . impotent . . . womanish . . . man-less . . . dog-child . . . pig-child." Since then she never looks at me – she never comes to me, rather she sleeps near a young boy of twenty who is lame but physically very strong. I have once seen them under the same quilt and they were going up and down.

CECIL: How pleasant! You have enjoyed enough.

ALVIN: No, only for some moments, later pain in my sex organ.

CECIL: Oh! You are a man without mercy – a man without love.

ALVIN:	Really, I have never felt the sense of love or mercy.
CECIL:	I also understand you have no friend.
ALVIN:	Right you are. Once I have fostered two parrots, Sweetish and Sweety. They were very nice and behaved very friendly towards me. They played with me. I used to give them puffed rice and milk to eat and they ate gladly. They used to address me "dear ALVIN, ALVIN . . . give to eat . . . come ALVIN . . . come ALVIN . . ."' But once I took them to a mango tree to let them eat some ripe fruits. They ate and chanted "dear ALVIN . . . " but later they fled leaving me alone while I called them saying, "o Sweetish . . . o Sweety . . . come here take milk and rice." But all was in vain and they never came back. A dog also resided near my hut and I used to give it food, especially meat and fish which he ate gladly. But suddenly, the dog escaped after some months and now lives near a big house where it eats meat and fish greater than given by me. Since then I am alone and I have never proposed friendship to anyone while I am always ready to create enmity.
CECIL:	It seems that you are prejudiced.
ALVIN:	No, I'm not prejudiced, rather I find the world without love – the world without God, and man has been divorced from his home, fear all around us.
CECIL:	You think that man is divorced but I don't agree with you.
ALVIN:	But I believe. I find it everywhere.
CECIL:	You don't know the world. You are frustrated because of a number of tragedies in your life.
ALVIN:	All have to divorce the world one day.
CECIL:	But in my neighbourhood all are unlike your parents.
ALVIN:	You are an ignorant man, like an ignorant army.

~ 20 ~

CECIL:	This is not a fact. They love their children and live with them. They think about them, they care for them and live with them.
ALVIN:	But in my neighbourhood all are like my parents – all children are like me.
CECIL:	You should try to know and ask them about their past.
ALVIN:	I do frequently.
CECIL	I understand their response will satisfy you.
ALVIN:	No. They say that whatever they do they have inherited from the past – from their ancestors.
CECIL:	But know it! All are like me in my neighbourhood – not whatever you say.
	[*Shows his wrist watch*]
ALVIN:	What is this?
CECIL:	This is a watch was given by my father to check time – to check actual time. This is the shirt was given to me by my father to wear. They loved me – they gave these things to me. Though I earn much more. It made me happy. It is a very costly shirt! This is the briefcase which I have bought with my own income . . .
ALVIN:	It seems that it says much about the actual place.
CECIL:	Not this watch, but my cell phone always indicates the location.
	[*Shows his mobile phone*]
ALVIN:	Show me too. It's one look only please. Let me see.
	[*Takes the phone and returns it*]
CECIL:	Missland is the name of this area. The mobile phone is indicating clearly.
	[*Shows the mobile phone to ALVIN*]
ALVIN:	It means it can also show the past home – our future home.

CECIL: No! This shows the present location only.

ALVIN: How can you know past and future?

CECIL: No one can tell about past and future.

ALVIN: Can this watch or this cell phone tell the actual time of your permanent departure from the world for an unseen home?

CECIL: No one can say.

ALVIN: This is totally meaningless, if it doesn't show it.

CECIL: This is a very costly item and a thing of great use. You do not understand its function. Anyone can contact anyone anywhere in the whole world with the help of this latest item. Let me show.

[Dials his wife and speaks to her image]

Hello . . . The train is late . . . See you later . . . Bye

ALVIN: But it fails to contact anyone of the past home and the future home.

[Long pause.

Off Stage. An announcement is heard. "Passengers, attention please! The Superfast Express . . . is running late by about an hour. The inconvenience caused is deeply regretted."]

CECIL: Alvin, please eat. The train is late.

[He passes a packet of food]

ALVIN: Okay.

[He sees it and refuses to take]

But it seems very spicy and tasty.

CECIL: Eat it.

ALVIN: It will cause acidity.

CECIL: It seems you suffer from acidity.

ALVIN: Yes.

CECIL: Tell me its symptom?

ALVIN:	Very dreadful! Intolerable pain in my stomach. It seems that the stomach has become a drum to beat. Dum . . . duma . . .
	[*Beats his stomach*]
CECIL:	How?
ALVIN:	The stomach becomes a balloon like a dead person's body in water for some days. I begin to sigh and then I roll on the ground because of intolerable pain in my abdomen. None comes and helps me be cured. But again and again I feel the same complication.
CECIL:	I mean you are unable to eat and digest such type of food.
ALVIN:	No! Most people are unable to digest spicy and oily food easily. I can digest, but . . .
CECIL:	What?
ALVIN:	This type of food is not available to me. I am a very poor man. But sometimes, some persons offer such type of food to me.
CECIL:	Do you also suffer from some other diseases?
ALVIN:	Yes! My eye sight is very dim. Hearing capacity is also very poor.
CECIL:	But my eye sight is very clear.
ALVIN:	Thus, you can see your past?
CECIL:	Heh . . . heh . . . no.
ALVIN:	And the future?
CECIL:	[*Calmly*] No!
ALVIN:	But you said that your eye sight is very clear.
CECIL:	I can see, but only the present.
ALVIN:	It seems that your eye sight is also dim like mine.
CECIL:	All are like me. They know only about the present.
ALVIN:	Have you studied in any university?

CECIL: Yes?

ALVIN: Which one?

CECIL: *Eduwell University.*

ALVIN: Where is this university located?

CECIL: In Heartland – in our neighbourhood – the best in the world.

ALVIN: What is your educational qualification?

CECIL: Aha double degrees! [*Very happily*] Master of Arts in Physics and Metaphysics!

ALVIN: You have studied in the world's best university. It is your opinion that the university provides the best education – awards the best knowledge.

CECIL: [*In a boasting manner*] All's right.

ALVIN: It means you and all other persons who have got education from that university know better than all others.

CECIL: [*In a boasting manner*] All's right.

ALVIN: I think you look at the past and present too.

CECIL: No one looks. How can I look?

ALVIN: All interprets the same.

CECIL: Yes!

ALVIN: I feel, in the earth-heart there is only one voice – the voice of [*Sigh*]. Everyone is weeping – everyone is dying – everyone is wailing. How much one possesses knowledge but fails to understand this matter. One does not know that he is nearing death. He is a permanent transient. He is isolated from his home which is unknown by him. One's knowledge secured from any university fails to understand all this. But let it go.

CECIL: I can . . .

           [*Extra long pause*]

ALVIN: You look like you are an officer.

CECIL:	Yes! I am working as a Managing Director in a well-known diamond factory of our country. [*Shows his Identity Card*]
ALVIN	Aha! Your salary is huge.
CECIL:	Yes! Very handsome! Knowing it you will be surprised. One million rupees per month! Plus . . . plus a kingly building, a dozen servants, several vehicles, ten days' paid leave in one month to enjoy with girl friends in luxurious hotels, an insurance for life, a gratuity, a bonus, and all other facilities are provided to me by the company.
ALVIN:	Aha! Your life is secured. You are immortal?
CECIL:	None is immortal.
ALVIN:	Insurance means.
CECIL:	If any causality occurs, compensation will be paid.
ALVIN:	To whom?
CECIL:	To my wife.
ALVIN:	Your wife will also get your life?
CECIL:	You seem a foolish man. No. Money . . . money to my wife.
ALVIN:	But you will get nothing.
CECIL:	This is natural.
	[*Long pause*]
ALVIN:	You don't live happily.
CECIL:	I'm very happy with what I have got – whatever has been given by God.
ALVIN:	Your employees are unhappy because you govern them. All beings want to remain free. That is their nature.
CECIL:	They are also very happy.
ALVIN:	You don't know them. They dislike you – they hate you.

CECIL:	No! They love me – they respect me.
ALVIN:	Where does your family live?
CECIL:	They live with me in the company's kingly building.
ALVIN:	How are they?
CECIL:	Very fine!
ALVIN:	Have you any beloveds?
CECIL:	That is not your business.
ALVIN:	I am not interfering with you. Please tell me. It is my desire to know.
CECIL:	Yes.
ALVIN:	How many?
CECIL:	Three . . . four . . . now . . .
ALVIN:	Not countable?
CECIL:	It is not a matter of discussion.
ALVIN:	How many?
CECIL:	Please talk to me within limits – with dignity and respect.
ALVIN:	I know they don't live with your family.
CECIL:	Yes, they don't live with me.
ALVIN:	Because you are afraid of your wife.
CECIL:	No.
ALVIN:	Why do they not live with you?
CECIL:	They live with their own families.
ALVIN:	You do not love them. So, they are separated.
CECIL:	I love them.
ALVIN:	You should live together but you are separated. [Surprisingly] Separated!
CECIL:	We used to meet them time to time.
ALVIN:	You meet them as we meet in stations.
CECIL:	No.

ALVIN: You should call them at home.

CECIL: Are they wives? So I will call them at my home. We do everything within boundaries.

            [*Longish pause*]

ALVIN: You live only with your family members. Do they not suffer from any disease?

CECIL: No! Never!

ALVIN: Do they digest spicy food like you?

CECIL: Yes!

ALVIN: Without complication?

CECIL: [*Very Proudly*] Yes, without complication!

ALVIN: But I feel that the world is ill. All are ill in their own ways. Acidity . . . anxiety . . . fever . . . fretting . . . depression . . . diabetes . . . headache . . . cancer etc. This is the death-land where only death exists, not life or love or joy – only sense of isolation, alienation, fear, loneliness, insecurity, mystery, and such and such all around us.

CECIL: But I feel joy and joy – the joy which welcomed me in my childhood never departed.

ALVIN: My findings are different.

CECIL: See the sign of pleasure on my face. [*Shows a family photograph*]

ALVIN: This smile is outward not inward. You have outward joy, but inward the sense of fear.

CECIL: See another picture. [*Shows the photograph of his wedding rituals, looking very smart*]

ALVIN: I see and find outward joy and inner fear. The same pleasure is not seen on your face as is seen in the photograph. Joy is decaying. The body is decaying. The body is nearing old age, and old age nears death.

CECIL:	See other photographs. The beauty of my house – which is gold and diamond coated. For security five licensed rifles to security guards in our house. No one can harm us.
ALVIN:	There is also a gas cylinder behind you in the same photograph.
CECIL:	It's very necessary for the kitchen.
ALVIN:	There is no oxygen.
CECIL:	What? I know.
ALVIN:	LPG. Very dangerous!
CECIL:	It's very useful.
ALVIN:	Dangerous . . . dangerous . . . one greatest fact! It will harm you. It will spoil your hope – everything. There are so many numbers of 'it', its agency. Emperors and monarchs surrender before its agency.
CECIL:	You are a fool. You want to say that danger resides in our kitchen.
ALVIN:	Danger is not only in your kitchens, rather all around us. Yes! With our birth.
CECIL:	How does one live here?
ALVIN:	It is a matter of consideration.
CECIL:	You should think about yourself.
ALVIN:	I know. For me too.
CECIL:	I also know. See some other items from my bag. [*Shows some things from his bag*]
ALVIN:	I see your salary certificate.
CECIL:	A handsome salary! But what is your income?
ALVIN:	My income is zero. Wherever I go, I beg. Whatever I beg, that is my income for the moment. Whenever I fall ill I cannot beg. Its result is that I remain hungry.
CECIL:	[*Sympathetically*] Oh! You remain hungry? Hungry?

ALVIN:	[*Very helplessly*] Yes! I always remain hungry!
CECIL:	[*Proudly*] I'm different. Quite different! What is not to me! Everything is to me! All employees in my company are happy.
ALVIN:	You have nothing.
CECIL:	You understand nothing.
ALVIN:	You lack everything, but you fail to understand anything.
CECIL:	I possess all things.
ALVIN:	You only lose and get nothing. All lose. No one gets.
CECIL:	No!
ALVIN:	Okay! Let it go. What is your age? Compare your body with the photograph in your hands.
CECIL:	Age is lost in any condition.
	[*Silently thinking*]
ALVIN:	Where are you going? Obviously, you're going to lose. Later it will be clear. Once, everything will be lost. All is absurd.
CECIL:	Oh! Am I nearing death? Life is absurd?
	[*Keeps silent*]
ALVIN:	You can see my clothes. [*Shows his old and dirty clothes*]
CECIL:	You don't wash it. Heh! How much dirt!
ALVIN:	I wash.
CECIL:	It is too dirty!
ALVIN:	I wash, but it becomes dirty.
CECIL:	Naturally.
ALVIN:	We do everything unnaturally.
CECIL:	No!
ALVIN:	Vividly . . . frequently . . .
CECIL:	I'm not an animal.

ALVIN: I'm feeling hunger and thirst. I want to go eat and drink, anywhere.

            [*Turns to go*]

CECIL: Listen to me. Have you money?

ALVIN: No.

CECIL: Take ten.

            [*CECIL hands ten notes to ALVIN, which he accepts*]

ALVIN: I'm going to eat.

            [*Goes slowly singing a "Man is a traveller, who comes and goes . . . "*]

CECIL: Okay.

            [*ALVIN leaves.*

            CECIL is alone. He watches ALVIN go.

            He looks at the items in his bags and briefcase.

            He hums the song sung by ALVIN which he was singing when he left]

            [*To himself*] Am I like Alvin? No I'm unlike him.

            Drinks water from his bottle.

            Begins to read a newspaper.

            Lights down.

ACT 3

Lights up.

ALVIN comes and sits near CECIL who is reading a newspaper.

CECIL: Firstly, please sing the song which you were singing on the way.

ALVIN: You will be thrilled having listened to the song – if you accept the facts of the world and the man.

CECIL: No!

ALVIN: I'm sure!

CECIL: I have listened to many songs in my life which I enjoy heartily.

ALVIN: You can't enjoy this song, rather a sense of fear, isolation, Insecurlty, alienation and loneliness will embrace you.

CECIL: Let it embrace, but sing the song which was very considerable.

ALVIN: If you want to listen, let me sing, and listen to it: [*Sings lyrically*]

> Man is a traveller who comes and goes;
> Coming and going leaves memories
> In the way – and passing his whole life
> In alienation, isolation,
> Fear, loneliness, mystery, and suspense;
> Placing life in a tragic-comic turn
> In this absurd, hateful, wide and large world
> –

> In this godless and joyless home of hope –
> Conflict of man against man forever –
> Man against himself – in chaos and menace
> –
>
> And in an irremediable exile.
> Man is a traveller who comes and goes.

CECIL: This is a song without meaning – a song of nonsense sung by a man of nonsense.

ALVIN: I have already told you that you will begin to thrill if you accept the facts in the song. Man lives in the world ignoring all these realities.

[*Longish pause*]

CECIL: Let it go. Today, you have eaten food and drunk water whole heartedly.

ALVIN: But in abdomen, not in soul.

CECIL: Very tasty food.

ALVIN: No!

CECIL: No? Why?

ALVIN: No taste!

CECIL: Why do you eat and drink?

ALVIN: Because I need to eat – I need to drink.

CECIL: You live to eat.

ALVIN: No!

CECIL: Why not?

ALVIN: I feel to do so, but not to live. None lives. Each one has to die. Death is fact. Life is absurd. Quite absurd! If I drink, now not but one day . . . unknown by me . . . I'll die. If I don't, I'll die at a time. Same to all . . .

CECIL: You have no knowledge.

ALVIN: Really, you have no knowledge. I have . . . natural . . .

CECIL:	What's all this? What do you say?
ALVIN:	I'm right.
CECIL:	I'm right.
ALVIN:	You're wrong.
	[*Puts his hands into his pocket and handles a knife which he doesn't take out*]
CECIL:	Consider your status . . . in which state you live.
ALVIN:	Yes, I know.
CECIL:	You don't know.
ALVIN:	O Cecil! A self-declared man of knowledge. Please think deeply . . . properly . . . whatever is in your bags . . . but something . . . not everything.
CECIL:	So many things are at my home – gold, diamonds, gems and pearls – everything.
ALVIN:	All, but not of you.
CECIL:	In fact.
ALVIN:	Is anything of your wife?
CECIL:	Mine are hers . . . hers are mine.
ALVIN:	The same thing to both?
CECIL:	Yes!
ALVIN:	Wonder!
CECIL:	"Mine" is a social and legal possession.
ALVIN:	But not natural! Only expectation!
CECIL:	My expectations have been ever fulfilled – whatever I wish and whatever I'll wish.
ALVIN:	You should be a minister.
CECIL:	Why?
ALVIN:	Why the post of the Managing Director? You're not the head.
CECIL:	There are more than 3,000 employees who work under me.

ALVIN:	Anyone above?
CECIL:	There is only one, not the 3,000.
ALVIN:	There is a minister above you . . . above him there is a law . . .
CECIL:	But I pay the salary to all 3,000.
ALVIN:	They give of their labour, losing their life, nearing the end of life.
CECIL:	They get my signature and seal.
ALVIN:	But your signature is within the law.
CECIL:	But there is no one under you.
ALVIN:	No one!
CECIL:	That is the difference.
ALVIN:	You must know some difference regarding death.
CECIL:	No!
ALVIN:	Items in your bag after death? Items in your home after death? Your family members after death? Children given birth by you after death? Your wife, after death?
CECIL:	My wife will possess all this. She will command all this.
ALVIN:	But after her death what will occur?
CECIL:	My children are men of great knowledge and understanding who will manage everything.
ALVIN:	You told me . . . all of your wife . . . all of yours . . . all of your children.
CECIL:	When I am living for me . . . and later . . .
ALVIN:	Life is for death.
CECIL:	I'm an optimist, so I think all will be good.
ALVIN:	Present is followed by future and future is fully dark. You are optimistic but you can't deny the facts.
CECIL:	Falling ill, doctors will cure me. Now I'm fine.

ALVIN:	Doctors treat ailments. Not life.
CECIL:	In my life . . . all goes well.
ALVIN:	No!
CECIL:	Yes!
ALVIN	You live in the realm of hope that is always unfulfilled. Life faces the most powerful agency . . . Death. Death is the permanent doctor.
CECIL:	I am rich, strong and healthy.
ALVIN:	Death ceases all.
CECIL:	Surely!
ALVIN:	Is your grandmother alive?
CECIL:	No.
ALVIN:	Did she like death?
CECIL:	No.
ALVIN:	Did she die as per her will?
CECIL:	No.
ALVIN:	So?
CECIL:	I've precious gems, jewels, gold and diamonds too. I can sell and buy anything if necessary. This will help me be cured if necessary – curable from the incurable.
ALVIN:	But not death to life.
CECIL:	To live long!
ALVIN:	Shorter or longer . . . but death is inevitable.
CECIL:	My bag is full of such things which you have never seen in your life. You can see it, if you will. [*Opens bag*]
ALVIN:	What are all these?
CECIL:	See for yourself. Aha!
ALVIN:	What things they are?!
CECIL:	This is so because you suffer.

ALVIN: Because of this?

CECIL: Yes.

ALVIN: This is the thing which you lack and I possess.

CECIL: You suffer only because of this reason.

ALVIN: Consider it! All is well, if one possesses all this!

CECIL: Yes, if a man possesses all this he can live happily.

ALVIN: You are fully off the track. What are you saying?

CECIL: That is the difference between you and me. So, you suffer and I live happily.

ALVIN: I suffer as I lack it, but why does a king suffer? Death also embraces a king.

CECIL: Death is for life. This is the cycle of the world.

ALVIN: You have also to follow the same cycle. You live in expectation, but expectations are never fulfilled.

CECIL: I don't wait for death. I live happily.

ALVIN: Be sure! In this way . . . you can't ignore death.

CECIL: I'm not a pessimist.

ALVIN: There is no use of the things which you have now after death? Be parcelled? Buried with one?

CECIL: No use . . . not to be parcelled . . . not to be buried!

ALVIN: There is no use for these kingly garments.

CECIL: This is the law of Nature.

ALVIN: Can you give something to me?

CECIL: Take it. [*Takes some items out of his bag and hands them to ALVIN who accepts*]

ALVIN: The entire bag!

          [*BLAIR returns and sits beside CECIL*]

BLAIR: Who is the man?

CECIL: He is my frie . . . nd, who is also to travel with us.

BLAIR: Do you know him?

CECIL:	No.
BLAIR:	This is not a matter. He is a traveller like us.
	[*Pause.*
	Off stage announcement: "Passengers, attention please! The Superfast Express . . . is running late by about an hour. The inconvenience caused is deeply regretted."]
CECIL:	Have you got medicine?
BLAIR:	Yes.
CECIL:	Have you taken?
BLAIR:	I have taken only the first dose.
CECIL:	Presently, how do you feel?
BLAIR:	Fine!
CECIL:	Okay. Sit here. I will return.
BLAIR:	Where are you going?
CECIL:	To buy cigarettes.
BLAIR:	Okay.
	[*CECIL goes to buy cigarettes.*
	ALVIN and BLAIR remain sitting]
ALVIN:	Very good! You are also to travel with Cecil.
BLAIR:	Yes.
ALVIN:	Perhaps you work in the same company.
BLAIR:	No. Only I work in a company. He is going with me on an adventure.
ALVIN:	You have a very heavy bag. You are bearing so many bags on a journey. It is not a good idea.
BLAIR:	Yes. But it is necessary.
ALVIN:	It is very tiresome. Man should remain burden-free. It helps to travel easily.
BLAIR:	There are some important and necessary things in these bags.

ALVIN:	Nothing is important in life. All is absurd as life is absurd.
BLAIR:	Neither am I a philosopher nor do I pass time discussing meaningless topics. Rather I need these things so I carry all this.
ALVIN:	Okay. Cecil has similar views.
BLAIR:	All this goes on in life.
	[*Long pause*]
ALVIN:	Cecil says that these are his bags.
BLAIR:	No, absolutely. No.
ALVIN:	Are all your bags?
BLAIR:	Except this little bag, all four are mine.
ALVIN:	Let him come here. I will ask him about it.
BLAIR:	Okay.
ALVIN:	Your faces are similar. It seems that you're his brother.
BLAIR:	No.
ALVIN:	Brother-in-law?
	[*BLAIR becomes angry. He scolds ALVIN*]
BLAIR:	Idiot. Don't cross the limit. We have given you a place to sit and you are abusing me.
ALVIN:	[*Agitated*] Don't be angry.
BLAIR:	[*Warning.*] Don't speak much more.
ALVIN:	What will you do? Look at my pocket. Do you see it? See a new and edgy knife.
	[*Takes out a knife and sets it to his hands as if ready to fight and attack.*
	CECIL returns]
CECIL:	What does he say?
BLAIR:	He says that I am your brother-in-law.
CECIL:	O vile man! Go away.

ALVIN:	Let me sit here.
CECIL:	We'll not let you sit here.
ALVIN:	Why?
CECIL:	This is our seat. We were sitting here before you. I offered a seat to you. You have not offered one to us.
ALVIN:	This is not your seat.
BLAIR:	This is our seat.
ALVIN:	This is my seat.
CECIL:	Never!
ALVIN:	Not!
CECIL:	Never . . . never!
ALVIN:	I'll certainly sit here.
CECIL:	You can't sit here because this is mine.
ALVIN:	This is mine!
CECIL:	No!
ALVIN:	You'll have to leave it.
CECIL:	No!
ALVIN:	I'm one, but stronger.
CECIL:	You can do nothing.
ALVIN:	I'll possess it.
CECIL:	You will have to leave it.
ALVIN:	Yes! I will sit here.
CECIL:	I'm entitled to this seat because I was sitting here before you. So the law will protect me.
ALVIN:	No law will protect you.
CECIL:	The Railway Consumer Act will protect us.
ALVIN:	But not the Natural Act!
CECIL:	The law is supreme.
ALVIN:	The law is not supreme. Nature is supreme.

CECIL: The station management will protect me.

            [*He holds onto his seat.*

            Both CECIL and BLAIR push at ALVIN]

ALVIN: Let me sit!

            [*Pushes back at them to take in an attempt to occupy the whole bench*]

CECIL: Never!

ALVIN: Just now I'll push you out from here.

            [*Begins to push forcibly.*

            CECIL and BLAIR continue to hold their seats very tightly.

            A television turns on at the end of the platform.

            They turn their attention to the screen.

            Voices from the television can be heard]

NEWSREADER: . . . The saddest road accident news of the year. All members, except one, of a family were killed in a road accident following the blast of a gas cylinder alongside the road. In the car, there were three children and two women along with the driver, the woman's husband and father of the children. The sole family survivor, Cecil, is currently out of town.

            [*CECIL watching the bulletin begins to weep bitterly*]

CECIL: Oh my God! Oh my God! I've lost everything. Now only woes and sorrows to me. I'll also die.

            [*Stands and leaves the bags*]

ALVIN: Why are you weeping?

CECIL: All are dead. I'll die.

            [*Stands in shock*]

ALVIN: What of the bags full of precious items here?

CECIL: Oh my God! Oh . . . my . . . God! I lost everything . . . Why will I live here? How will I live?

BLAIR:	Oh Cecil! Silence! Oh!
	[*BLAIR pacifies CECIL.*
	Silence]
ALVIN:	Oh!
BLAIR:	All goes meaningless. All is absurd.
	[*Off stage announcement: "Passengers, attention, please! The Superfast Express . . . is about to arrive at platform one."*]
ALVIN:	Hold your seat. This seat is not good. This seat is for aliens. I do not want to sit here. I want to go to my permanent home. I will not pass any more time here.
BLAIR:	You can sit here.
ALVIN:	Thank you Cecil, thank you Blair, thank you very much. The way has been paved. I will depart for home. The train is just about to arrive. I am departing for my permanent home. You should escape from here because the police may arrest you charging that you pushed me onto the track.
BLAIR:	Oh! What?
ALVIN:	[*Smilingly, jumps onto the railway tracks committing suicide*] Oh my God, oh . . . my . . . God!
	[*Off stage. The sound of a train arriving is heard.*
	An announcement follows. "Passengers, attention, please! The Superfast Express . . . has arrived on platform one. Passengers with tickets are requested to board."]
BLAIR:	Oh Alvin! Oh Alvin! Oh my God! Oh my God . . . !
CECIL:	Oh my God! The police will arrest us. Oh my God! Oh my God! Oh my God! Save us! Save us! Save us!
BLAIR:	O Cecil! Escape from here as soon as we can, leaving all this because the policemen are coming.

Oh my God! Oh my God! Save us! Save us! Oh my God! Oh my God! Oh my God!

They go quickly, leaving their luggage.

Lights fade during which the song *"Man is a traveller who comes and goes" is played from various directions. An announcement is made. "Passengers, attention please! The Superfast Express . . . will be delayed by half an hour because of a person on the tracks. Any inconvenience caused is deeply regretted."*

.

www.ingramcontent.com/pod-product-compliance
Lightning Source LLC
La Vergne TN
LVHW051713080426
835511LV00017B/2886